A Pet's Life

Guinea Pigs

Anita Ganeri

Heinemann Library
Chicago, Illinois

www.heinemannraintree.com
Visit our website to find out more information about Heinemann-Raintree books.

To order:

☎ Phone 888-454-2279

🖳 Visit www.heinemannraintree.com to browse our catalog and order online.

© 2009 Heinemann Library
an imprint of Capstone Global Library, LLC
Chicago, Illinois

Customer Service: 888-454-2279

Visit our website at www.heinemannraintree.com

Printed and bound by South China Printing Company Ltd

13 12 11 10 09
10 9 8 7 6 5 4 3 2

Library of Congress Cataloging-in-Publication Data
New edition ISBN: 978 14329 3392 0 (hardcover) – 978 14329 3399 9 (paperback)
The Library of Congress has cataloged the first edition as follows:
Ganeri, Anita, 1961-
  Guinea pigs / Anita Ganeri.
     v. cm. -- (A pet's life) (Heinemann first library)
Includes bibliographical references (p.   ).
Contents: What is a guinea pig? -- Guinea pig babies -- Your pet guinea
pig -- Choosing your guinea pig -- Preparing your cage -- Welcome home
-- Guinea pig play-time -- Feeding time -- Cleaning the cage -- Growing
up -- A healthy guinea pig -- Old age.
  ISBN 1-4034-3996-6 (hardcover) -- ISBN 1-4034-4272-X (pbk.)
  1. Guinea pigs as pets--Juvenile literature. [1. Guinea pigs. 2. Pets.] I. Title. II. Series.
  SF459.G9G36 2003
  636.9'3592--dc21
                      2002151594

Acknowledgments
The author and publishers are grateful to the following for permission to reproduce copyright material:
Alamy p. **20** (© Petra Wegner); © Capstone Global Library Ltd. pp. **27** (Mark Farrell), **4**, **9**, **10**, **11**, **12**, **13**, **16**, **17**, **18**, **19**, **21**, **23**, **24**, **25** (Tudor Photography); Chris Honeywell pp. **14**, **15**; Dorling Kindersley p. **6** (Paul Bricknell); RSPCA p. **22** (Angela Hampton); Shutterstock p. **8** (© carsthets); Warren Photographic pp. **5**, **7**, **26** (Jane Burton).

Cover photograph of a guinea pig reproduced with permission of iStockphoto (© Eline Spek).

The publishers would like to thank Judy Tuma for her invaluable assistance in the preparation of this book.

Every effort has been made to contact copyright holders of any material reproduced in this book. Any omissions will be rectified in subsequent printings if notice is given to the publisher.

Contents

Some words are shown in bold, **like this**. You can find out what they mean by looking in the Glossary.

What Do Guinea Pigs Look Like?

Guinea pigs are small, furry animals with tiny ears and tails. There are many different **breeds** and colors of guinea pigs. Some have short fur, and some have long fur.

A guinea pig with short fur, like this one, is best for a first-time pet owner.

This picture shows the different parts of a guinea pig's body. You can see what each part is used for.

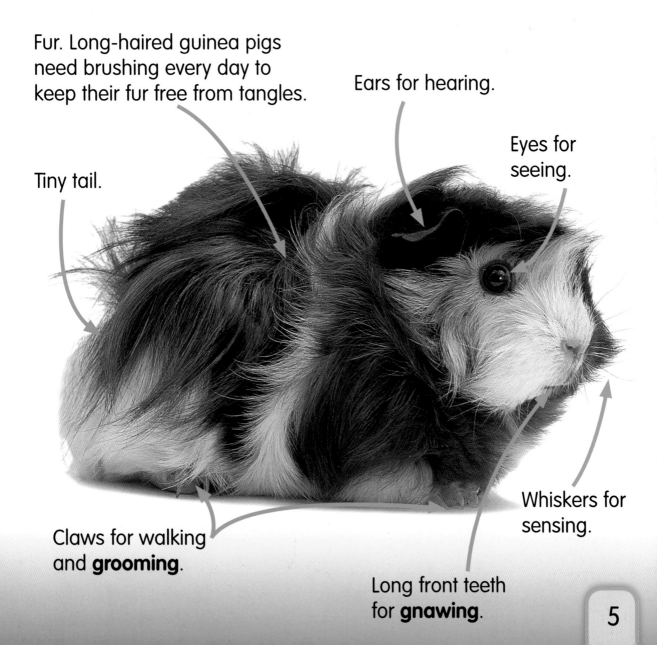

Fur. Long-haired guinea pigs need brushing every day to keep their fur free from tangles.

Ears for hearing.

Eyes for seeing.

Tiny tail.

Whiskers for sensing.

Claws for walking and **grooming**.

Long front teeth for **gnawing**.

Guinea Pig Babies

Guinea pig babies are called pups. A mother guinea pig has from one to six pups in a **litter**. The pups are born with lots of fur and their eyes are open.

The guinea pig pups drink their mother's milk.

A female guinea pig can have up to 25 pups a year. It is best to keep males and females apart.

The pups are old enough to leave their mother when they are about three weeks old. Then they are ready to become pets.

Choosing Your Guinea Pigs

Animal shelters often need good homes for guinea pigs. You can also buy guinea pigs from good pet stores or guinea pig **breeders**.

Guinea pigs like company. It is unkind to keep just one as a pet. Choose two males or two females from the same **litter**.

A healthy guinea pig should be lively and interested in you.

Choose chubby guinea pigs with shiny coats. Check that their ears and eyes are clean, and that their teeth are not too long.

Your Guinea Pigs' Cage

Your guinea pigs need a large cage to live in. Put a layer of unscented hardwood **shavings** on the floor, and a clean pile of hay for bedding.

Do not use a cage with a wire floor. This will hurt your guinea pigs' feet.

For two guinea pigs, the cage should measure at least 18 inches high, 24 inches wide, and 3 to 6 feet long.

Keep the cage in a warm place in your house. Be sure it is away from loud noises and safe from other pets.

Welcome Home

You can bring your guinea pigs home in a cardboard box. At home, put them in their new cage. Then leave them alone for a few hours so they can settle in.

Make sure that your carrying box has holes in it so that your guinea pigs can breathe.

Stroke your guinea pig gently and talk to it softly.

Guinea pigs are quite shy. Be gentle when you pick your pet up. Put one hand under its bottom and the other hand around its shoulders.

Play Time

Guinea pigs are easily scared, so always approach their cage slowly. They need lots of space to play and exercise.

Guinea pigs do not often jump or climb.

Check toys for sharp pieces that could hurt your guinea pigs.

Guinea pigs love to play hide and seek and run through tubes. Put some boxes, or other objects on the floor for your pets to explore and hide behind.

Feeding Time

You can buy special guinea pig food from a pet store. Guinea pigs also like to eat chopped fresh fruit and vegetables. They also need fresh hay.

Your guinea pigs need lots of **vitamin C**. They can get this from raw apples, carrots, cabbage leaves, spinach, and oranges.

Make sure that your guinea pigs always have fresh drinking water. Put a water bottle in their cage.

You should feed your guinea pigs every morning and evening. Put their food in heavy bowls that will not tip over. Hay and water should be available at all times.

Cleaning the Cage

You can help to keep your guinea pigs healthy by keeping their cage clean. Remove any wet bedding, old food, and **droppings** every day.

You also need to wash out the water bottle and food bowls every day.

Give the cage a complete scrubbing and be rinse it well. Allow it to dry before you put your pets back in.

Once a week, empty the cage and give it a good cleaning. Put in some fresh unscented hardwoood **shavings** and bedding. Wash your hands when you are done.

Growing Up

Guinea pigs grow up quickly. When a male guinea pig is full grown, it will weigh about two pounds. Female guinea pigs are a little smaller than males.

Adult guinea pigs are about 8 to 10 inches long.

If your guinea pig whistles,
it can mean that it is hungry,
thirsty, or happy to see you.

Guinea pigs talk a lot. They squeak, tweet,
chatter, or whistle when they know they
are going to be fed.

Healthy Guinea Pigs

Your guinea pigs will stay healthy if you take care of them. If your guinea pig does not eat, seems tired, or starts sneezing, it may be sick.

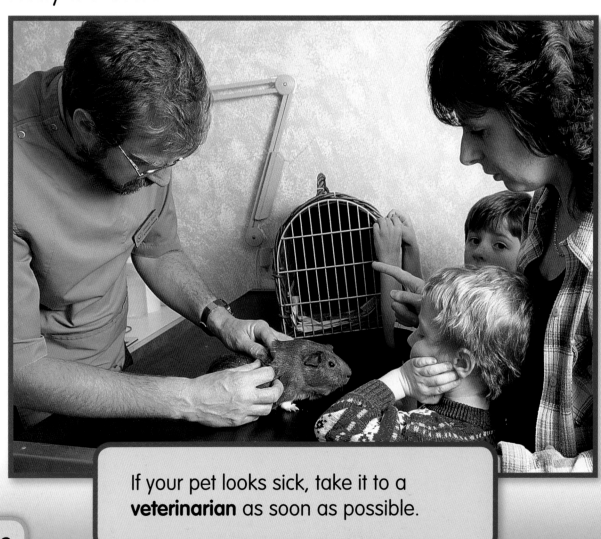

If your pet looks sick, take it to a **veterinarian** as soon as possible.

A guinea pig's front teeth and claws can grow too long. Give your guinea pigs a wooden **gnawing** block to wear their teeth down. A veterinarian can trim their claws.

If your guinea pigs' teeth grow too long, they will not be able to eat properly.

Your Pet Guinea Pigs

Guinea pigs are fun to keep as pets. You must be a good pet owner and care for them properly.

Your guinea pigs will depend on you for all of their needs.

Write a list of what your friend should do and leave it by the guinea pigs' cage.

Your guinea pigs need food and water every day. If you are going on vacation, ask a friend or neighbor to look after your pets.

Old Age

If you look after your guinea pigs, they may live for up to seven years. Check them every day to make sure they are healthy

Guinea pigs hate the cold. They need to be kept warm, especially in winter.

Older guinea pigs still need to be cared for every day. They still enjoy being held and cuddled, too.

Caring for your guinea pigs will help you learn how to treat animals properly.

Useful Tips

- Always wash your hands before and after touching your pets, their food bowls, and their cage.

- Guinea pigs **groom** themselves. But you need to brush long-haired guinea pigs every day to stop their fur from getting tangled. Use a soft toothbrush or a baby's hairbrush.

- If your guinea pig holds its head to one side and cannot walk in a straight line, it may have an ear **infection**. Take it to a **veterinarian**.

- If your guinea pigs start pulling out each other's fur, it means that they are bored. Make sure that they get plenty of exercise.

- Don't let guinea pigs run around your house alone. They may chew electric power cords and get hurt.

Fact File

- Wild guinea pigs live in South America.

- Guinea pigs are named after Guiana, one of the South American countries where they live.

- Guinea pigs are **rodents**. They belong to the same group of animals as hamsters, squirrels, mice, and rats.

- Male guinea pigs are called boars and females are called sows, just like real pigs.

- Adult guinea pigs need dry food and hay every day, plus a small amount of fresh fruit and vegetables.

Glossary

animal shelter place where lost or unwanted animals can be looked after

breeder someone who raises animals

breed group of animals of the same type

droppings waste from the body

gnaw chew and bite

groom gently brush and clean your guinea pigs' fur. Guinea pigs also groom themselves.

infection sickness

litter baby guinea pigs born at the same time

rodent animal that gnaws, such as a mouse, rat, squirrel, or hamster

shaving very thin slice of wood

vitamin C goodness in food which guinea pigs need to stay healthy

veterinarian doctor who cares for animals

More Books to Read

An older reader can help you with these books.

Barnes, Julia. *Pet Pals: Pet Guinea Pigs*. Strongsville, OH: Gareth Stevens Publishing, 2006.

Boyer Binns, Tristan. *Keeping Pets: Guinea Pigs*.

Chicago, IL: Heinemann Library, 2006.

Miller, Heather. *This is What I Want To Be: Veterinarian*. Chicago IL: Heinemann Library, 2004.

Salzmann, Mary Elizabeth. *Perfect Pets: Goofy Guinea Pigs*. Edina, MN: Abdo Publishing Company, 2007.

Small Pet Care: How to Look After Your Rabbit, Guinea Pig, or Hamster. New York: Dorling Kindersley Publishing Inc., 2005.

Index